T0142598

THE
A-Z
OF
YOU AND ME

by
Iris McClain

AuthorHouse™
1663 Liberty Drive
Bloomington, IN 47403
www.authorhouse.com
Phone: 1 (800) 839-8640

© 2018 Iris McClain. All rights reserved.

No part of this book may be reproduced, storedww in a retrieval system, or
transmitted by any means without the written permission of the author.

Published by AuthorHouse   07/31/2020

ISBN: 978-1-5462-5594-9 (sc)
ISBN: 978-1-5462-5595-6 (e)

Library of Congress Control Number: 2018908187

Print information available on the last page.

Any people depicted in stock imagery provided by Getty Images are models,
and such images are being used for illustrative purposes only.
Certain stock imagery © Getty Images.

This book is printed on acid-free paper.

Because of the dynamic nature of the Internet, any web addresses or links contained in this book may have changed
since publication and may no longer be valid. The views expressed in this work are solely those of the author and do not
necessarily reflect the views of the publisher, and the publisher hereby disclaims any responsibility for them.

authorHOUSE®

<u>Purpose</u>

This R.E.D. Book series, The A to Z of You and Me, consists of 26 books designed to discuss the very delicate subject, sexual abuse particularly among children. Even though I wrote these books about 8 years ago, it is fitting to introduce them now with the recent scandal about the coach who abused at least 150 victims, most if not all were children. Not to mention those who may have remained silent for fear or embarrassment.

Also, the MeToo Movement has infiltrated the news and our children hear it. No doubt, we need a way to discuss this sensitive subject with our young, vulnerable children, (any age group) who may be targeted so as to avoid their future or continued victimization.

Introducing the USTOO Movement to give a voice to the child victims and the adults who were victimized as children. #USTOO

These books provide a healthy avenue to discuss abuse. For those who have been victimized, hopefully the books will help them cope with the stigma, guilt and embarrassment the perpetrator oftentimes impresses upon them.

Let's give the little ones a voice #USTOO. These books are:

Age Sensitive

Age Adaptable

Educational

Interactive

Short and Concise

Timely

About R.E.D. Books

Each R.E.D. book is designed to teach, educate, entertain and pave the way for communication between parents/caretakers/guardians and the children entrusted with their care. Parents/caretakers/guardians are encouraged to read the books with the children. Each R.E.D. book presents sensitive subjects in a positive, fun way.

The books are designed to help parents discuss very delicate subjects with their children from infancy and beyond. All ages will enjoy reading these books, over and over again.

It takes courage and boldness to discuss delicate subjects; therefore, look for the R.E.D. books to help you.

Each Book provide an atmosphere that is conducive to learning and enjoying life 24-7. They are unified and are not divided by race, nationality, age, language and/or family ties. They represent the fun, positive side that rests within each and every one of us.

Enjoy!

Personal Dedication

This series of books is dedicated to my mother and sister, who always encouraged me to write.

This book belongs to

_____

A is for Abuse

<u>ABUSE</u>

Abuse is any unwanted action that a person may do to you, verbal or physical. It can be a touch, a kiss, what they say or how they look at you. "YELL, SCREAM, RUN, TELL… if someone tries to abuse you".

If anyone abuses you, you should tell immediately.

I will tell if you...

ABUSE ME

Verbally
Sexually
Physically
Emotionally

A is for Accept

ACCEPT

Accept means to take what is given.

Children are taught not to accept gifts from strangers.

Don't accept a gift from anyone, if they ask you not to tell your parent/caretaker about it.

Do not accept a ride from anyone.

I will not...

ACCEPT

gifts without my parents' approval

A is for Adults

ADULTS

Adults are older persons. They can be a relative, neighbor or a friend. Children are taught to respect and obey adults. Respect and Obey does not mean allowing them to touch us unhealthily.

Relatives: a mother, father, sister, brother, aunt, uncle, grandmother, grandfather, cousin, the husband, the wife, step and/or blended family members.

Friends: friends of the family, school teachers, coaches, doctors, nurses, bus drivers, babysitters, day care providers, dentists, principals, Bible teachers, counselors, preachers, dance instructor, tutor, piano teacher.

Neighbors: people who live near us or other relatives we visit.

A is for Allow

<u>A L L O W</u>

Allow means to let. Children, young ones must not allow anyone to touch them or say things to them that make them feel uncomfortable.

If an adult says bad things about your parents, to befriend you, do not allow that adult to be your friend.

If an adult allows you to do things they know your parents do not agree with (smoking, drugs, dating, drinking, driving) do not allow that adult to be your friend. They could be befriending you to keep you from telling if they abuse you.

I will not…

ALLOW

Anyone to make me feel uncomfortable
about obeying my parents

A is for April

<u>APRIL</u>

April is the 4th month.

April is Sexual Assault Awareness Month.

Many people participate in different activities to help bring an end to sexual assault.

A is for Awareness

<u>AWARENESS</u>

Awareness is when you know about something.
It is also the ability to feel the danger of a situation.

<u>DISCUSS</u> with your child . . .

Abuse

Accepting Gifts

Adults in your child's daily life

Allowable behavior

April Activities they can participate in

Awareness

Practice with your child…

Situations

Yelling

Screaming

Discussing Abuse

About the Author

Iris McClain is the mother of four and grandmother of 2, who resides in Prince George's County Maryland. She has always been interested in reading, education and helping others. She believes there are a lot of adults who, by choice, are living in silence about the sexual abuse they endured as a child.

She believes only God's Kingdom will eradicate all child sexual abuse. Nevertheless, if this series of books can prevent 1 child from experiencing abuse, then the purpose of writing them has been served.

She is the Author of <u>Two Sisters One Breast</u>. To order, text 240-601-8165.

To pre-order volumes B – Z, email me at <u>A-Zofyouandme@gmail.com</u>

Printed in the United States
By Bookmasters